THE GREATEST ATHLETES OF ALL TIME

ADAM GRANT

SUE MACY

ERIC MENDELSOHN

MOLLY T. JACKEL

WAYNE COFFEY

JERE LONGMAN

JACOB MARGOLIES

JOE LAYDEN

SCHOLASTIC INC.

New York   Toronto   London   Auckland   Sydney
Mexico City   New Delhi   Hong Kong

Copyright © 1999 by Scholastic Inc.
All rights reserved. Published by Scholastic Inc.
Printed in the U.S.A.

ISBN 0-439-05711-6

SCHOLASTIC, READ 180, and associated logos and designs are
trademarks and/or registered trademarks of Scholastic Inc.
LEXILE is a trademark of MetaMetrics, Inc.

9 10   2 3   06 05 04

TABLE OF CONTENTS

Who is the greatest athlete of our century?

It's not an easy question. There are hundreds of superstars in the world of sports. How could you possibly decide what makes an athlete *the greatest*?

Is it natural talent, or hard work?

Can you measure greatness in statistics? Or is it something you can't put a number on?

Is it a matter of courage? Is the hero the one who plays in pain, the one who keeps fighting, no matter what?

Or is it creativity? Some athletes enter a sport that has been played for generations. Then they change it. They do things nobody else could even think of doing.

Maybe it's leadership that makes an athlete truly great. Great leaders inspire everyone else to play at a higher level.

Or maybe it's showmanship. Some stars are all about dazzle. It's who they are, as much as what they do. After all, sports are meant to entertain.

Or is real greatness produced by some combination of all these things?

In this book, eight sportswriters offer their opinions about the answers to these questions. Then they've made their picks for the greatest athlete of the twentieth century. So here's the big question: Which of these sports stars do *you* think is the greatest?

He bragged that he was the greatest. Then he proved it again and again.

MUHAMMAD ALI

BY ADAM GRANT

For my money, the greatest athlete of the twentieth century is Muhammad Ali. He had heart, ability, creativity, and showmanship. He also had the most important gift of all—the courage to be himself.

In the early 1960s, most boxers weren't much more than street bullies. Many were like heavyweight champion Sonny Liston, who had learned to box in prison. They spoke awkwardly. They were barely educated.

Then a new kind of fighter arrived like a lightning bolt. He was handsome and charming. He was funny and quick-witted. He bragged about himself in rhyming verse.

"This is the story about a man," he once chanted. "With fists of fury and a beautiful tan./ He talks a lot and boasts indeed/ Of a power punch and blinding speed."

He was always confident, even cocky. He

5

predicted how many rounds it would take him to knock out his opponents. Then he made his predictions come true. Whenever he got the chance, he told the press, "I am the greatest!" Then he'd go into the ring to prove it.

This was Cassius Clay. In 1960, he came back from Rome, Italy with a gold medal in his hand. He'd won the Olympic tournament as a light heavyweight. And he was ready to take the world of professional boxing by storm.

Clay had been preparing to be a champion for a long time. He was born in 1942, in Louisville, Kentucky. He'd set his sights on the heavyweight championship when he was 12. Nothing, and nobody, was going to stop him. That included restaurants that wouldn't serve him because he was black—even when he had his gold medal around his neck. It included that "old bear" Sonny Liston. It included the press.

Reporters said he was all talk. They called him the "Louisville Lip." They thought he was loud and arrogant. They claimed he would never last. He needed to be taught a lesson in the ring, they said.

Clay just kept on going. "This is America," he said. "I don't have to be who you want me to be. I can be whoever I want." It seems like a simple statement now. For a black man at that time, it was an incredible act of courage.

From 1960 to 1967, Clay put on a show. The sports world had never seen anything like it. In 1964, he shocked the world by defeating the "unbeatable" Sonny Liston. The heavyweight championship was his.

Over the next few years, he held off every challenger. "I'm pretty, I'm young, and I can't possibly be beat!" he reminded his fans and opponents. "I am the greatest!"

In the ring, there was nothing like him. He was big and strong. His hands and feet moved so fast you could hardly see them; he lived up to his motto "Float like a butterfly, sting like a bee." He had amazing balance and endurance. He could take punches that no one else could.

Still, it was Clay's courage outside the ring that truly made him great.

Clay grew up in the South in the 1940s and 1950s. He had faced racism and hatred. After he won the heavyweight crown, he knew the time had come for him to make his voice heard.

He had something to show the world. An African-American man could stand up for what he believed in, even if it wasn't popular.

The day after Clay beat Liston, he announced that he had joined a religion called the Nation of Islam, commonly known as the Black Muslims. He changed his name to Muhammad Ali, which meant "worthy of praise."

The press said that Ali was insulting the public. They claimed that the Nation of Islam was an anti-white cult. Ali insisted that it was a brand of the Islamic faith, not a cult. Black Muslims were not anti-white, he said. They were pro-black. He challenged America to accept him, his faith, and his new name.

Then he went back to the boxing ring. As he rolled through his opponents, the public began to accept him again. "One thing about America," he said. "You stand up for your rights and people will eventually adjust."

In 1967, Ali risked everything once again. America had gone to war in a country in Asia called Vietnam. Men were being drafted every day. When Ali received his draft notice, he refused to go. The war, he said, was against his religion.

This time, Ali lost everything. He had to go to court. He was found guilty of evading the draft. The press called him a traitor. At the height of his career, he was stripped of his title as heavyweight champion of the world. And he was banned from his sport.

For three years, Ali fought for his rights in court. He lost nearly all his money. He tried to stay in shape.

Finally, in June 1970, the court made a new decision—Ali was not guilty. He announced that he would start boxing again as soon as possible. By this time, he was 28 years old. He had lost three important years of his fighting career. The press said he would never be a champion again.

Once again, Ali proved them wrong. Over the next five years, he beat many powerful, younger champions. These fights were some of the greatest battles in boxing history.

He won two out of three fights with Joe Frazier. He split two fights against Ken Norton.

In 1974, Ali squared off against heavyweight champion George Foreman in Zaire, Africa. Foreman was a towering, terrifying fighter and *no one* gave Ali a chance. Sports commentator Howard Cosell said, "I don't think Ali can beat George Foreman. Maybe he can pull off a miracle. But I can't conjure that."

Ali had no trouble imagining a miracle. And he

made one happen. He took shot after shot to the body and kept coming back. By the eighth round, Foreman had tired. Ali knocked him out with a combination to the head.

Ali was champion of the world once again.

There are three amazing qualities that place Ali in a class by himself. As a boxer, he dominated his sport like no one ever has. He won the world heavyweight championship three different times in his 20-year career.

As a showman, Ali had no equal. He had a dazzling smile and a great sense of humor. For example, in 1962, when he fought ex-champ Archie Moore, he chanted, "Archie been living off the fat of the land/ I'm here to give him his pension plan./ When you come to the fight, don't block the door/ Cause you'll all go home after round four."

Ali's charm and style hypnotized the world. When he started, only serious boxing fans cared about the sport. By the time Ali was through, people all over the world were interested in the sport. And Muhammad Ali was one of the most famous and loved people on earth.

As a human being, Ali is even more impressive. He has used his celebrity status to help people across the globe. He traveled to the world's poorest, most desperate regions. He knew that wherever he went, his presence gave people pride and hope. He showed the world that a proud African-American man could succeed. He could do it without apologies. He could do it without help.

If you ask me, professional athletes today often seem too worried about their bank accounts to take a stand. A little conflict might cost them a TV commercial. Would Michael Jordan or Ken Griffey, Jr., risk their fortunes for a political belief? Maybe. Maybe not. But *all* athletes could learn a thing or two from Muhammad Ali.

Adam Grant, a writer and musician, grew up in New York City. He is a lifelong Yankees, Knicks, Rangers, and Ali fan.

In 1988, Adam worked at Yankee Stadium in the scoreboard control booth. His most memorable sports moment came when Yankees owner George Steinbrenner personally called to yell about a mistake Adam had made.

Accomplishments: Muhammad Ali

Golden Gloves middleweight champion: 1960

Olympic light heavyweight champion: 1960

Heavyweight champion of the world:
1964–1967, 1974–1978, 1978–1980

Career record (1960–1981): 56 wins, 37 by
knockout; five losses

Admitted into U.S. Olympic Hall of Fame: 1983

Admitted into International Boxing Hall of
Fame: 1990

She raised the roof in the Women's National Basketball Association.

CYNTHIA COOPER

BY SUE MACY

I'd like to say that basketball star Cynthia Cooper is the greatest athlete of the twentieth century. But I can't.

It's almost impossible to rank athletes. There just isn't enough information. Men's sports have been thoroughly covered in newspapers and on TV. For example, you can still see tapes of Muhammad Ali's fights. But until recently, women's sports were not often filmed or reported in the media.

Besides, choosing *the* greatest athlete celebrates just one person. To me, it seems more important to highlight all athletes who've actually *changed* their sports. And in that way, "Coop" ranks right up there with the greatest athletes of all time— including all-around star Babe Didrikson Zaharias, tennis great Martina Navratilova, and track legend Jackie Joyner-Kersee.

Cynthia Cooper was not a well-known player when she joined the Women's National Basketball

Association (WNBA) in 1997. She had played on two championship college teams and had won two Olympic medals. But the spotlight usually focused on her flashier teammates. Plus, she had spent most of her pro career in Europe, far from American fans.

It seems now that Coop was standing in the shadows. Maybe she was just waiting for her chance to shine. People who remembered her from college thought of her as a dependable team player. She could get the ball to a star shooter. She could help stop opponents from scoring.

But by the time the WNBA started up, Coop had changed her game. "I never felt like I had given all I was capable of giving to one of my teams," she said. "I wanted to be one of those people who took the clutch shots and carried teams on their shoulders."

Coop ended up carrying more than her team on her shoulders. She set the standard for achievement in the WNBA. Her "raise the roof" cheer—with both her hands pumping up toward the sky—seemed to suggest the limitless possibilities for women's pro basketball and women's sports in general.

Cynthia Cooper was born in Chicago, Illinois.

She grew up in the Watts section of Los Angeles, California. She learned a lot about strength from her mother, Mary Cobbs. Cobbs raised eight children on her own.

Cooper has always played sports. And she has always played them *hard*. At age 10, she was a shortstop on a softball team bound for the play-offs. In one game, she misjudged a line drive and ended up with a broken nose.

The experience didn't discourage her. Instead, it taught her to tough things out. "Your body's going to do what your mind tells it to do," she says. "And if my mind tells me I can play, then I can do it. I can take an elbow and get up. Or play that last minute of the game when I can barely walk. Or when I'm exhausted."

In high school, Cooper ran the hurdles. She also played volleyball, softball, and badminton. She didn't take up basketball until she was 16. She had seen a young woman dribble a ball down the court, do some fancy ball handling, and make a lay-up. "Just like that, I said, 'Oooh, wow, I want to play like that someday,'" she remembers.

She was new to the game. But Cooper won a scholarship to the University of Southern California (USC). There, she played alongside

Basketball Hall of Famer Cheryl Miller. Their team won two national titles.

Cooper also played on the 1988 United States Olympic basketball team, which won the gold medal. And she played on the 1992 team, which took the bronze.

But in the late 1980s, the U.S. had no professional basketball league for women. Those who wanted to earn a living playing the game went overseas. Coop spent 11 seasons playing for European teams. She learned to speak Italian and Spanish in the process.

In 1997, Cynthia returned to the U.S. And she couldn't have returned at a better time. The WNBA was just getting started.

The new league was getting lots of attention. It also had the support of the National Basketball Association (NBA). But if the players didn't dazzle the fans, the league would fail.

For starters, the WNBA's directors were looking for superstars. They chose three: Sheryl Swoopes, Lisa Leslie, and Rebecca Lobo. But things didn't go as planned.

Lobo was a crowd favorite. But she was young, and her game needed to mature.

Leslie was a great shooter. But she spent a lot

of time and energy on her second career: modeling.

And Swoopes learned that she was pregnant before the season started. She wouldn't be able to play until her baby was born. By then it would be late summer. And most people expected that her Houston Comets would be stuck in last place.

League officials felt they had to do something. So they assigned Cynthia Cooper to the Comets. Coop had put up some good numbers playing in Spain and Italy. She had averaged 35.5 points per game in 1995–1996. And her average hadn't dropped below 26 in the last eight seasons.

That was just a hint of what she could do.

Coop became the WNBA's greatest all-around player. By the end of the season, she had placed in the top 10 in scoring, assists, steals, shooting accuracy, three-point accuracy, free throw accuracy, and minutes played.

The 5'10" guard led the league in scoring with 22.2 points per game. She was the first player to reach 600 points. In 1998, she became the first player to reach 1,000 points.

She set the individual game scoring record three games in a row. By the time she was done, she had a high of 44 points.

At the free throw line, she hit 86.4 percent of

her shots. With Coop leading the way, the Houston Comets won the first WNBA championship.

Cooper was a leader off the court as well. A few months before the first WNBA season started, she learned that her mother had breast cancer. Coop helped her mother fight the disease. She researched treatment information on the Internet. She put together an all-natural diet for her mother. She tried to arrange her practice schedule around her mother's chemotherapy sessions.

Cooper also became a spokesperson for *Concept: Cure*, a breast cancer awareness program. And she started Coop Hoop for Kids. This group supports breast cancer research and programs focusing on children's cancer and inner-city education.

When the second WNBA season began in 1998, Cooper was no longer standing in the shadows. She was starring in commercials. She was singing the league's "Join In" theme song. She was rapping about women's basketball. In one ad she walks past two sweaty guys playing a tough game of one-on-one. She gives them her biggest compliment: "Yo," she says, "you all play like girls."

Coop was now guarded by two, or sometimes three, opponents. Still, she led the league in points per game and three-point field goals. She'd spent 12 years as a pro. Now this "overnight" success was leading women's basketball into the next century. Her contributions to the game were not lost on her fans.

At one game in Houston, they held up a sign that said it all: "SUPER COOPER, U DA MA'AM!"

Sue Macy is the author of *Winning Ways: A Photohistory of American Women in Sports*; *A Whole New Ball Game: The Story of the All-American Girls Professional Baseball League;* and *Play Like a Girl*.

Accomplishments: Cynthia Cooper

Olympic medalist: 1988 (gold), 1992 (bronze)

Led European league in scoring, 8 times in 10 seasons

WNBA Most Valuable Player: 1997, 1998

WNBA scoring leader: 1997 (22.2 points per game), 1998 (22.7 points per game)

Member WNBA Championship team (Houston Comets): 1997, 1998

He gave his heart and soul to baseball—and his life to people in need.

Roberto Clemente

BY ERIC MENDELSOHN

When Roberto Clemente was growing up in Puerto Rico, he was too poor to buy sports equipment. So he and his friends wrapped a rock in old rags. They made a bat out of a tree branch. And whenever they could, they played baseball.

Roberto's mother often scolded him for missing dinner. She demanded to know where he had been. His answer was always: "Playing baseball, Mama." One night Roberto's mother lost her temper and threw his bat into the fire.

Roberto pulled the bat out of the flames. He was silent for a long time. Finally he said, "Mama, I believe that God wants me to play baseball."

Three decades later, Roberto Clemente had made it to the top of his sport. He was wealthy beyond his dreams. His fame stretched from Puerto Rico to Pennsylvania. And yet, he never forgot his roots.

Roberto spent his money and his time helping

the people he loved. His talent and his determination made him a great athlete. But it was his compassion that made him the greatest athlete of all time.

Roberto Clemente was born in 1934, in the Puerto Rican city of Carolina. He quickly became the best baseball player in the neighborhood. He also excelled at track-and-field events.

When he was 20, Clemente heard about tryouts for American major league teams. He showed up and caught the eye of Al Campanis, an agent for the Brooklyn Dodgers. Clemente was throwing strikes from deep in center field. He ran 60 yards in 6.4 seconds. (The world record was 6.1 seconds.)

Campanis sent the other players home. And he offered Clemente a $10,000 bonus to sign with the Dodgers. It was the largest bonus ever offered to a Hispanic player.

Roberto accepted and headed north to play in the big leagues. Before long he was traded to the Pittsburgh Pirates.

Clemente quickly became the Pirates' star player. He punched out line drives with ease. He ran the bases aggressively. But Clemente's most spectacular plays came in the field. He used his blinding speed to chase down ball after ball. He made impossible, leaping, stretching catches. Sometimes, he would even climb the back field fence to stop a home run ball. Often his dazzling grabs ended with a perfect throw to home plate to cut off a base runner. Plays like these eventually won Clemente 12 Golden Glove awards for best right fielder.

For a long time, the Pirates had struggled at the bottom of the league. But in 1960, with Clemente's help, the team was turning things around. In one game, baseball legend Willie Mays smashed a line drive to right field. Clemente raced for the ball and dove—right into the right-field wall. He climbed to his feet with blood gushing from his head. He raised his glove high in the air. He had the ball. The crowd yelled the Pittsburgh battle cry: *Arriba, Arriba!*—Spanish for "Let's go!"

The Pirates went on to beat the New York Yankees in the World Series.

Clemente found that life in the big leagues wasn't easy for a Hispanic player. Sometimes people made fun of his accent. Journalists refused to recognize his talent. "What does it take for a Latin player to be truly recognized?" he wondered.

But he just kept working harder than ever.

Clemente once said, "A country without idols is nothing." And Roberto gave Puerto Rico a hero worth cheering for. Between seasons he went back home to play on the local winter team. He signed thousands and thousands of autographs. After all, he said, the fans "pay my salary, and they work hard for what they earn."

He also did what he could for kids. He raised money for children with disabilities. He visited sick kids in the hospital. He even planned a great "Sports City" for the youth of Puerto Rico.

By 1971, Clemente had earned a lot of respect. But on the field, the best was yet to come. According to sportswriter Roger Angell, that season Clemente played "a kind of baseball that none of us had ever seen before." Clemente was "throwing and running and hitting at something close to perfection," Angell said.

Roberto carried the Pirates into their second World Series. This time they went up against the Baltimore Orioles.

The 1971 series was Clemente's breakthrough. He owned the series. He hit in every game, batting .414 for the series. He racked up 12 hits, two homers, and four key RBIs. In the field, he stole hits from batter after batter.

Sportswriter Dick Clark said that Clemente was "the best ballplayer in the World Series, maybe in the whole world."

Clemente was named Most Valuable Player. At the awards ceremony, he spoke in Spanish. He asked for his parent's blessing. And he spoke about his connection to "the poor people, the workers, the minority people, the ones who suffer."

There was one more milestone for Clemente: In 1972 he became only the eleventh player in major league history to get 3,000 hits.

That winter, Roberto was enjoying the off-season with his family in Puerto Rico. Two days before Christmas, disaster struck the Central American nation of Nicaragua. An earthquake hit the capital city of Managua. It killed and injured thousands, and left thousands more homeless.

Money, medicine, and clothing began pouring into Nicaragua. The people of Puerto Rico quickly sent three planeloads of supplies.

Clemente went to work organizing relief shipments. But he heard that only some of the supplies were reaching the Nicaraguan people. Politicians were stealing from the shipments.

Clemente was furious. "The stealing will stop,"

he declared. He decided to ride with the next shipment. "They would not dare to steal from Roberto Clemente," he said.

The flight was delayed for many hours as mechanics worked on the old plane. Finally it took off. As the plane rose over the ocean, it began to shake. Then the engines exploded. The plane crashed into the waters around Puerto Rico. Clemente's body was never recovered.

After Clemente's death, he was immediately inducted into the Baseball Hall of Fame. Baseball commissioner Bowie Kuhn said about Clemente, "He was so very great a man, as a leader and humanitarian, so very great an inspiration to the young, and to all in baseball, and to the people of his proud homeland, Puerto Rico."

That's why I think that Roberto Clemente is the greatest athlete of all time.

Eric Mendelsohn teaches writing in New York City and holds the world record for the short indoor nap.

ACCOMPLISHMENTS: ROBERTO CLEMENTE

Won four separate National League batting titles (1961, 1964, 1965, 1967)

National League's Most Valuable Player (MVP) in 1966

MVP in the 1971 World Series

Won the Gold Glove award (for defensive play) 12 consecutive years

National League All-Star 12 times

Hit .317 over 18 seasons, collecting 3,000 hits, including 240 home runs

First Hispanic player admitted to the baseball Hall of Fame, in 1973

Martina and Billie Jean served up greatness, on the court and off.

Billie Jean King
Martina Navratilova

By Molly T. Jackel

Tennis great Billie Jean King was my first hero. When I knew she was playing, I'd march in front of the TV and order my dad and brother to change the channel.

Baseball or football just wasn't good enough. I wanted to watch a real athlete. And to me, Billie Jean was the real thing. She was graceful, strong, smart, and competitive. She didn't need a coach telling her what to do every five seconds. And she didn't disappear when she stepped off the court. She showed up again and again, fighting to give women athletes chances they'd never had before.

So there's no question that Billie Jean King is a great hero. But is she really the greatest athlete? I'm torn. I'd like to shout, "Of course she is!" But I have to admit, there's someone who's stronger, faster, and better—Martina Navratilova.

And that is high praise. Billie Jean King racked up an impressive record during two decades of competition. She won 695 matches. Thirty-nine of those wins came in Grand Slam finals—at the U.S. Open, the French Open, the Australian Open, or Wimbledon. At the time, only one player, Margaret Court, had ever won more.

King also became the first woman in any sport to earn more than $100,000 in a single season. She was number one in the world five times, from 1966 to 1972. She ranked in the top ten for 17 years, beginning in 1960.

But to me, King's stats are just the icing on the cake. Here's the cake: Almost single-handedly, she made sure that women players got paid.

When Billie Jean started out, women earned less than one-third the prize money that men earned. In 1973, King decided that that had to change. So she demanded that the U.S. Open give women equal pay the following year. If they refused, she said, she would skip the tournament.

Their answer? They paid, and King played.

Billie Jean also convinced her fellow players to form a union, the Women's Tennis Association (WTA). The WTA still helps players negotiate with tournament officials and TV networks.

But King's biggest victory for women's tennis was on the court. In 1973, Bobby Riggs challenged Billie Jean to a match. Riggs was 55, and he'd done most of his winning back in the late 1930s. But he wanted to show that an old man could beat the best woman ever. That, he said, would prove that women didn't deserve as much money as men.

At first, King turned down the challenge. She had never claimed that women could beat men. She was just pointing out that women players attracted big crowds. And that's why they deserved equal pay.

While King waited, someone else took Riggs up on his offer—and lost. He started bragging that any man could beat any woman. And Billie Jean had to take the challenge.

Their match was a media circus. Thirty thousand fans showed up. More than 50 million watched on TV.

Billie Jean won in straight sets: 6-4, 6-3, 6-3. It was probably the most influential tennis match ever. You should have seen the girls and women out on the courts the next day!

King inspired a whole new generation of tennis players. And at the crest of the new wave was Martina. Navratilova left her home and family behind in Czechoslovakia when she was still a teenager. Her government had refused to let her play outside her homeland. Her talent was

MUHAMMED ALI

At the 1996
Olympics in
Atlanta, Georgia,
Muhammad Ali
was selected
to light the torch
at the opening
ceremonies.

In May 1965, Ali knocked out Sonny Liston in the first
round. He had also beat Liston the year before,
capturing the heavyweight championship of the world.

Cynthia Cooper

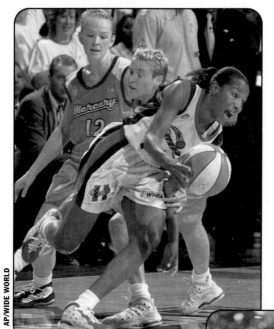

Houston Comets' star Cynthia Cooper during Game 2 of the 1998 WNBA Championships. The Comets beat the Phoenix Mercury, 74–69 in overtime.

The Comets beat the Mercury two games to one in the 1998 series, winning their second straight title. Coop celebrated with her "raise the roof" cheer.

ROBERTO CLEMENTE

Clemente racked up the 2,996th of his 3,000 career base hits against the Philadelphia Phillies in 1972.

Known as the greatest right-fielder to ever play the game, Clemente made a spectacular catch during a 1970 game against the New York Mets.

BILLIE JEAN KING

AP/WIDE WORLD

In 1973, former tennis great Bobby Riggs challenged King to a match, claiming that he could beat any woman star. King humiliated him— and took home the $100,000 prize.

MARTINA NAVRATILOVA

GARY M. PRIOR/ALLSPORT

Martina delivering a power shot during Wimbledon in 1994. Navratilova won a record nine singles titles at Wimbledon. In fact, she won more singles titles than any other player in history.

PELÉ

Pelé spent most of his career—from 1956 to 1974—with the Santos of Brazil. He is shown here in 1976, during a short, three-season stint with the New York Cosmos.

JACKIE JOYNER-KERSEE

Jackie throwing the javelin during the heptathlon at the 1992 Olympics in Barcelona. She won two medals at this Olympics.

Despite an injury, Jackie won the 100-meter hurdles in the heptathlon at the 1996 Olympics in Atlanta.

At the world championship in Athens in 1997, Joyner-Kersee seemed to take flight during the qualifying round of the long jump.

WAYNE GRETZKY

Playing for the Los Angeles Kings, Gretzky moved the puck past the Washington Capitals' goalkeeper during a game in 1989. Gretzky's trade to the Kings the year before had involved five players and $15 million.

MICHAEL JORDAN

They don't call him Air Jordan for nothing! Here's Jordan during the NBA Finals against the Utah Jazz in 1998. It was Jordan's sixth NBA title.

AP/WIDE WORLD

wasting away, so she fled to the United States. At 18, she was alone in a brand-new country. She didn't know if she would ever return.

Martina adjusted pretty fast. Before long, she was mowing down her competitors like grass. No one before her had won as many matches or titles, or as much prize money. No one was stronger, faster, or more intense. The "ladylike" sport of tennis was a thing of the past.

Martina wasn't well-liked back then. She was aggressive and muscular. She played like a man, people said. Somehow, she was threatening to men and embarrassing to women. Even after Billie Jean, women weren't supposed to be so strong, so aggressive, so athletic.

Martina played a lot like Billie Jean. She attacked the net at every chance, while everyone else waited for the ball at the baseline. Her serves were like precision cannonballs, and her overhead shots made teeth chatter.

Navratilova was good and fast from the start. But when she went into a slump, she started a serious training routine. She hired a nutritionist and a personal trainer. She studied how her body worked. Then she put the information to good use. She pumped iron. She ran a few miles every day. She jumped rope, played basketball, and practiced three hours a day. She turned winning into a science.

When she got her body in top shape, she was unbeatable. She won a record nine singles titles at Wimbledon. In 1984, she won 74 matches in a row. People are still chasing that record. And Martina's level of fitness is still the standard in women's sports.

I admire Billie Jean for taking a stand. Nobody has done more to give women athletes what they deserve. But does that make her a better athlete? King's achievements off the court don't make her better than Navratilova was on the court.

And let's not forget what Martina's done for women's sports. She created a new standard of fitness and health. She helped the public accept big biceps and bulging leg muscles on a woman athlete. She made it okay for women to work hard in order to win.

Martina made strength, stamina, and health a number-one priority. No female athlete had ever done that before. Today you can find fit women on magazine covers everywhere. Now it's acceptable to be strong and feminine at the same time. For that, we can thank Martina Navratilova.

And why do we love sports anyway? It's not to

follow what athletes do in their spare time. We're looking for excitement, grace, and glory on the court and on the field. Martina brought us all that—and more.

To me, Billie Jean will always be a hero. But Martina is the greatest athlete of all.

Molly T. Jackel is co-author of *WNBA Superstars*. She likes to imagine that she is the superflyweight boxing champion of Brooklyn. The author lives in Massachusetts, but she will never be a Boston Red Sox fan.

Accomplishments: Billie Jean King

Major singles titles: Wimbledon (1966, 1967, 1968, 1972, 1973, 1975); French Open (1972); Australian Open (1968); U.S. Open (1967, 1971, 1972, 1974)

Founded Women's Tennis Association, 1973

Named one of *Life* magazine's "100 Most Important Americans of the Century"

Accomplishments: Martina Navratilova

Major singles titles: Wimbledon (1978, 1979, 1982, 1983, 1984, 1985, 1986, 1987, 1990); French Open (1982, 1984); Australian Open (1981, 1983, 1985); U.S. Open (1983, 1984, 1986, 1987)

Record holder, career singles tournament victories: 158

He was the greatest player in the world's most popular sport. He was also the most humble.

PELÉ

BY WAYNE COFFEY

It happened more than 40 years ago. But that doesn't matter. Magic, after all, is magic.

A man runs like the wind across a huge, green field. He wears a familiar yellow jersey. The number 10 and the word *Brazil* are on the back.

Suddenly, he races forward even faster. The ball stays with him, as if attached by a string. He squeezes through two defenders. He bounces the ball off the turf, then off his chest. It falls to his right foot, and he rockets it past the diving goalkeeper.

The man's name is Edson Arantes do Nascimento. But millions of people around the world know him as Pelé.

Pelé played what he called "the beautiful game" for more than 20 years. During that time, he repeated that scene more than 1,200 times.

He was the best soccer player ever to strap on shin-guards. And soccer is the most popular game on earth. That means he was the best player in the most widely played game. We all respect Michael Jordan, Jackie Joyner-Kersee, and Muhammad Ali. But who else can top that? That's why Pelé is the world's greatest athlete.

Pelé grew up in a small Brazilian town called Tres Coracoes. His father was a minor-league soccer player. The family was always poor.

Pelé dropped out of school in fourth grade. That was not uncommon among poor Brazilian families. He helped bring in money by shining shoes, and he spent all his free time playing soccer. He played barefoot with a knot of old socks for a ball.

At 15, Pelé left home to begin his professional soccer career. Before long he was the best player in Brazil. And that was just the beginning.

In 1958, Pelé exploded onto the international scene at the World Cup of Soccer. The World Cup is like the World Series, the Super Bowl, and the Olympics all rolled into one. It is the world championship of the world's most popular game. And it happens only once every four years.

Pelé was 17. And he was competing in one of the most high-pressure events in sports.

He made his mark in a tight quarterfinal match

against Wales, scoring the game's only goal. In the semifinals, he struck again, scoring three more goals against France. In the finals he pumped in two more goals, as Brazil beat Sweden. He was called a genius.

He would spend the next two decades playing better and better. Fans claimed he was the greatest soccer player the game had ever seen.

Pelé scored 1,281 lifetime goals. That's almost a goal a game in the highest levels of world competition. That's about the same as hitting a home run in every post-season baseball game. It is an amazing feat.

Pelé also had explosive quickness and mind-boggling ball control. Yet what truly set him apart was his feel for the game. Like a chess master, he would play four, five, or six moves in advance.

His peripheral vision was amazing. He could see 30 percent more than most of us from the corners of his eyes. So he saw possibilities other players did not.

He didn't just play the game. He seemed to sense the flow of a match. He painted it, using the field as his own private canvas.

Often, Pelé didn't even need the ball to practice his art. Instead, he'd run away from the action and the ball. He'd go to the exact right spot at the exact right time. If the pass came at the right time, he'd score a goal. "He plays a game that nobody else can understand," a teammate said.

But when Pelé heard compliments, he'd just smile and shrug. "This doesn't make me proud," he once said. "It makes me humble. This is a talent that God has given me."

Pelé's modesty is yet another reason to salute him. These days star athletes have egos that are bigger than their muscles. Their biggest mission is to draw attention to themselves.

On October 1, 1977, Edson Arantes do Nascimento played the last beautiful game of his career. It was held at Giants Stadium in New Jersey. It was a match between the Cosmos and the Santos of Brazil.

Pelé's fans packed the stadium —in fact, the game had been sold out for six weeks. Thirty-eight nations tuned in to the broadcast of the match. About 700 reporters showed up at Giants Stadium to write about it. And boxing great Muhammad Ali arrived to pay his respects.

It was a game his fans would never forget. During his career, Pelé had played for both the Cosmos and the Santos. So for this match, he did something no professional athlete had ever done before. He played half the game with one team, and the other half with the other team. And fittingly, Pelé scored a goal—his 1,281st.

After the game, Pelé took the microphone and spoke to the crowd. He thanked all his fans for sharing "this greatest moment of my life."

Then he went on. "I want to take this opportunity to ask you to pay attention to the young of the world, the children," he said. "We need them so much. I want to ask you . . . to say with me three times, 'Love . . . Love . . . Love.'"

The fans did as he asked. The stadium rocked with a chant not heard before or since. It is hard to imagine any other athlete asking for—and getting—such a response.

Pelé's talent was matched only by his humility. And that is why I think that the little man with the big name, Edson Arantes do Nascimento, is the greatest athlete the world has ever seen.

Wayne Coffey is a sportswriter for the *New York Daily News* and the author of more than 30 books. He has played soccer for many years, but he has never once been mistaken for Pelé.

Accomplishments: Pelé

Led Brazil to World Cup championship: 1958, 1962, 1970

South American Player of the Year: 1973

North American Soccer League MVP: 1976

Inducted into National Soccer Hall of Fame: 1993

Scored 1,281 lifetime goals

She was the fittest of the fit in the most grueling event in sports.

JACKIE JOYNER-KERSEE

BY JERE LONGMAN

At age 36, Jackie Joyner-Kersee showed up at the 1998 Goodwill Games in New York. She had decided to take one more shot at the heptathlon. She was surrounded by doubters. Many people thought she wouldn't even finish the event.

The heptathlon is the most grueling competition in sports. It's designed to test an athlete's all-around skills. Over a period of two days, a field of iron-women compete in the hurdles, the shot put, the javelin, the 200-meter sprint, the high jump, the long jump, and the 800-meter run. Joyner-Kersee had won two Olympic gold medals in the event. She was widely known as the world's greatest female athlete.

But her career was ending. Some thought she would embarrass herself in a field of young athletes. And on the last night, she was exhausted. The weather was brutal—hot and humid. But when Jackie crossed the finish line of the 800 meters, she had yet another victory. She retired wearing her crown as the queen of track and field.

"I just kept plucking away," Joyner-Kersee said. "Never once did I say I was going to quit. I kept in my mind that I could still do it."

This is why she gets my vote as the world's greatest athlete. No one has ever had more determination than Jackie Joyner-Kersee. No one has succeeded so dramatically when nearly everyone expected failure. And few athletes have given back to their sport as much as they have taken out of it.

Jackie Joyner was born in one of America's poorest cities, East St. Louis, Illinois. But from the day she was born, her family wanted her to succeed. Her grandmother named her after Jacqueline Kennedy, the wife of President John F. Kennedy. She wanted her granddaughter to grow up to be "the First Lady of something," she said.

Of course, no one knew Jackie would become the First Lady of track and field. But she took an interest in the sport early on. When she was little, she and her two sisters walked to a nearby park and scooped sand into potato chip bags. They came back and dumped it into a homemade jumping pit. Then they learned to long jump off the front porch.

The other kids in the neighborhood called Jackie a tomboy. She liked to wear pigtails and cutoff jeans and a T-shirt. She played every sport that was offered at the local recreation center.

Soon, the phone was ringing off the wall. Coaches everywhere wanted Jackie to play on their basketball, softball, and volleyball teams.

"The only thing I ever asked is that she learn to stand on her own two feet. Whatever decisions she made, she made with her heart," said Al Joyner, Jackie's father. "I never figured her career would turn out like this."

In 1978, everyone quit calling her a tomboy and began just calling her an athlete. It was her sophomore year of high school. She led Lincoln High in East St. Louis to state titles in basketball and track.

The next season, the rules changed at Lincoln High. Now the girls got the gym right after school. And the boys had to return to practice basketball after dark.

Jackie went on to college at the University of California in Los Angeles. There, she met a track coach named Bobby Kersee and later married him. With her husband as a coach, she would rack up six Olympic medals. In four Olympics, she won three gold medals, one silver, and two bronzes.

At the 1984 Summer Olympics in Los Angeles, it was Jackie's brother, Al Joyner, Jr., who won the triple-jump and took home a gold medal.

But four years later, in Seoul, South Korea, Kersee outdid her brother. She took home two gold medals—one in the heptathlon and another in the long jump.

At the 1992 Summer Games in Barcelona, Spain, Jackie won the heptathlon again. There was no doubt now that she was the greatest female athlete of her generation.

But her spirit showed even more in defeat than in victory. Sometimes she would get an asthma attack at a meet. She would have to wear a mask on the track to help her breathe. It was impressive just to see her finish an 800-meter race.

At the 1991 world championships in track and field in Tokyo, Japan, Jackie injured her leg during the 200-meter race. She was taken away on a stretcher. But she insisted on speaking with reporters before leaving the track.

During the 1996 Atlanta Olympics, she was hit with another injury. A pulled hamstring forced her to withdraw from the heptathlon. At the last minute she decided to compete in the long jump. But she found herself in sixth place after five jumps. Then, on her final jump, she leaped from sixth place to third and took home a medal.

"I was so happy to get the bronze because it had been so tough," Jackie said. "Because of the injury, I really had to try to focus and stay positive."

In retirement, Joyner-Kersee will work as a sports agent and as the owner of a sports marketing firm. And she is committed to building a community center in East St. Louis. She wants to give other girls opportunities that she had.

Jackie's records will probably be broken. But she will stay dedicated to helping others follow in her path. To me, that's greatness. As Jackie Joyner-Kersee's husband Bobby Kersee said, "Track and field is not just losing a great athlete. It is losing a great person."

Jere Longman is the chief Olympics correspondent for *The New York Times*. He has covered every winter and summer Olympics since 1988. He has run three New York City Marathons. But he is still trying to crack the top 8,000.

Accomplishments: Jackie Joyner-Kersee

Olympic medalist, heptathlon: 1984 (silver); 1988 (gold); 1992 (gold)

Olympic medalist, long jump: 1988 (gold); 1992 (bronze); 1996 (bronze)

World Champion, heptathlon: 1987, 1993

World Champion, long jump: 1987, 1991

World record holder, heptathlon: 7,291 points in 1988

"The Great One" dominates the record books of the National Hockey League.

WAYNE GRETZKY

BY JACOB MARGOLIES

Hockey fans around the world know him simply as "The Great One." For 20 years, Wayne Gretzky has ruled the National Hockey League (NHL). He has led his team to the NHL title four times. In the process he has shattered every scoring record in the history of the game.

No athlete dominates the record book of his sport the way that Gretzky does. Imagine how his scoring feats might translate to other sports. He won seven straight scoring titles in the 1980s. During that time, he averaged just under 200 points (goals plus assists), a year. That was 50 percent better than the second-leading scorer.

Gretzky tore apart the single-season goal record just as Mark McGwire broke baseball's home run mark. But over time, McGwire hasn't come close to Gretzky's feats. He would need to repeat as home run king for the next five years to match The Great One.

Every time Gretzky scores a goal or an assist, he breaks his own record. There's never been a basketball player who has dominated both scoring and playmaking like that. Suppose you could combine Michael Jordan's scoring and Magic Johnson's passing in a single player. Then you might have someone with skills equal to Gretzky's.

Gretzky was headed for greatness from an early age. He grew up in Ontario, Canada, where nearly everyone plays hockey. Gretzky's father had his son playing the game at the age of two. By five he was skating six hours a day.

When Gretzky was only 10, he scored 378 goals in one season. Hundreds of articles about him appeared in magazines and newspapers. Four years later, Gretzky left home and began playing in a junior hockey league.

In 1978 Gretzky joined the Edmonton Oilers. At 17, he was quiet and shy. But over the next 10 years, he would turn the Oilers into one of the greatest teams in hockey history.

Gretzky became a superstar practically overnight. There were other players who were bigger, stronger, and faster. There were others who shot the puck harder than Gretzky. But nobody could match his skill and creativity on the ice.

A great goal scorer in the NHL might score 50 goals in a season. In Gretzky's third full season with Edmonton, he scored 92 goals. He also had an incredible ability to find open teammates in front of the net. One year in Edmonton, Gretzky had an amazing 163 assists.

With his awesome instincts, Gretzky made it all look easy. He shook defenders by turning on a dime. He got to the puck before anyone could get near him.

Gretzky once explained his secret. "I get a feeling about where a teammate is going to be," he said. "A lot of times, I can turn and pass without even looking. You do not need a hard shot to score goals. You just have to be quick and bang it in there as fast as possible."

Gretzky raised the Oilers to a higher level. The Oilers were new to the league. But with Gretzky on the ice, they beat teams that had dominated professional hockey for many years. Gretzky led the Oilers to the Stanley Cup in 1984, 1985, 1987, and 1988. He was named hockey's Most Valuable Player eight years in a row.

Eventually, Edmonton had to let The Great One go. They needed money. So they traded Gretzky to the Los Angeles Kings after the 1988 season. The trade involved five players and 15 million dollars. It was one of the biggest in NHL history.

Gretzky's arrival electrified L.A. The southern California city had never had much interest in hockey. But it welcomed the blond, handsome Gretzky as though he were a movie star. Suddenly new fans were flocking to see the Kings.

Gretzky put on a dazzling show. And hockey fever spread across the Sun Belt. Before long, the NHL had new teams in Florida, Texas, North Carolina, California and Arizona. Without Gretzky's star power, this expansion would not have been possible.

In Los Angeles, Gretzky broke the only scoring record that was not yet his. Gordie Howe held the career record of 801 goals. It was similar to Babe Ruth's magic number of 714 career home runs.

Howe had been the game's dominant player in the 1950s and 1960s. His mark had stood for three decades. Fans thought it would never fall.

When Gretzky scored goal number 802, Howe was there to congratulate him. "It's a true honor to have my record broken by a man like Wayne Gretzky," Howe said. "I couldn't be prouder."

Today Gretzky plays for the New York Rangers. He's one of the oldest players in the NHL. But he's still one of the league's leading stars.

The Great One has dominated hockey for 20

years. The NHL record book says it all.

Most Goals: Wayne Gretzky.

Most Assists: Wayne Gretzky.

Most Points: Wayne Gretzky.

Most Games Scoring Three or More Goals: Wayne Gretzky.

Most Consecutive 40-or-More-Goal Seasons: Wayne Gretzky.

Most 100-or-More-Point Seasons: Wayne Gretzky.

Now that's greatness. That's The Great One.

Jacob Margolies is a journalist who lives in Brooklyn, New York. He has written three books about sports, *Basketball Great: Kareem Abdul-Jabbar*; *Hank Aaron: Home Run King*; and *The Negro Leagues: The Story of Black Baseball*.

Accomplishments: Wayne Gretzky

NHL Most Valuable Player: 1980, 1981, 1982, 1983, 1984, 1985, 1986, 1987, 1989

Lady Byng Trophy winner: 1980, 1991, 1992, 1994

NHL scoring leader: 1981, 1982, 1983, 1984, 1985, 1986, 1987, 1990, 1991, 1994

NHL career scoring leader: 885 goals, 1,910 assists (after 1997–98 season)

MVP of Stanley Cup Playoffs: 1985, 1988

His talent took him a long way. Working harder than anyone else took him even further.

MICHAEL JORDAN

BY JOE LAYDEN

Who's the world's greatest athlete? Well, one rises high above the others. He's so far above, in fact, that "Air" is his nickname. That could only be Michael Jordan.

A lot of people know that Michael can fly. He's led the Chicago Bulls to six National Basketball Association (NBA) championships. He's the most famous athlete on the planet. Even kids in Europe, Asia, and Africa hang Michael's posters on their walls. They wear jerseys with Michael's number—23—splashed across the back. They pretend they can dunk like Michael.

They all want to be like Mike.

What makes Michael Jordan so special? How has he won ten NBA scoring titles and two Olympic gold medals? Why was he picked for five Most Valuable Player (MVP) awards? How does he keep playing so well as he gets older? Is it talent, ambition, or both?

The truth is this: Michael has physical gifts that allow him to walk across the sky. Still, no athlete has ever worked harder. No one has ever pursued greatness the way he does.

Basketball was not always easy for Michael. His coach once cut him from the team at Laney High School in Wilmington, North Carolina.

He was just a skinny, 15-year-old kid then. But the experience hurt him. It also made him hungry. "I vowed never to let that happen again," he once said.

He was true to his word. Michael made the varsity team the next year. By graduation, he was one of the country's top high school players.

At the University of North Carolina, Michael continued to blossom. As a freshman, he led the Tar Heels to the National Collegiate Athletic Association (NCAA) title in 1982. He even hit the winning shot in the championship game.

He's been a great clutch player ever since. Some athletes fade when the game is on the line. Michael doesn't. He loves pressure. He wants the ball.

After college, Michael started flying through the NBA. Not since Julius Erving—the legendary Dr. J—had anyone soared so high. Michael was a

6'6" guard with great leaping ability. His flying dunks could bring fans to their feet and opponents to their knees. And he was deadly with the jump shot, which made him almost impossible to defend.

He is the best all-around player the NBA has ever seen—as well as its most entertaining.

At first, Michael was a one-man show. He led the NBA in scoring four times in his first six seasons. He also won the NBA Slam Dunk Championship twice.

Still, he wasn't satisfied. Michael was hungry for a championship ring.

In 1991, he got his wish. He led the Bulls to their first NBA title. A second title followed in 1992. A third came in 1993. Michael was named the play-off MVP all three years. In the 1993 NBA finals against the Phoenix Suns, he was unstoppable. He set an NBA record by averaging 41 points per game.

By now, Michael was on a roll. He was the most popular athlete in the world. He was a smart businessman who'd made millions by endorsing products. He'd helped to make basketball the hottest sport on the planet. Still, for Michael, the biggest test was yet to come.

It happened one month after the 1992–1993

season ended. Michael's father was murdered. The tragedy made Michael question his entire life.

The next October, he shocked fans by announcing his retirement. "The death of my father made me realize how short life is," he said. "I want to give more time to my family."

But that wasn't the only reason he was giving up hoops. "I have nothing left to prove in basketball," he told reporters. "I have no more challenges."

The best basketball player in the world wanted a new challenge. So, he announced he was taking up baseball. He signed a contract with the Chicago White Sox.

Michael's fans were stunned. How could anyone switch sports at the age of 30? What was he trying to prove?

Many people didn't know the facts. Michael had played a lot of baseball with his father. His boyhood dream was to be a big-league ballplayer. It had been his dad's dream, too. "This is something that has been in the back of my mind for a long time," Michael said. "It's something that my father and I talked about often."

Michael worked hard at his new career. He became a pretty good minor-league baseball player. But he wasn't good enough to make the major leagues. After two years, he got the urge to return to basketball. He put away his cleats and laced up his Air Jordans.

Many people questioned Michael's comeback. He was 32 years old. Surely he would be slower.

Michael was determined to prove everyone wrong. He shook off the rust and led the Bulls to NBA titles in 1996, 1997, and 1998.

At this point, Michael was one of the oldest players in the league. But it didn't matter. Maybe he wasn't quite as quick as he once was. Maybe he couldn't dunk as well. But he was definitely smarter than ever.

He developed new moves. He had a fade-away jump shot that no one could block. He could draw the defense in his direction, then pass to an open teammate at the last second. In many ways, he was better than ever.

Michael was named MVP for the fifth time in 1998. He kept thriving under pressure. In the last seconds of game six of the NBA finals, the Bulls desperately needed a basket. They turned to Michael Jordan. With a great crossover dribble, he left his defender sprawled near the foul line. Then he made a 15-foot jump shot. It was the last of his 45 points.

The basket gave the Bulls an 87–86 victory over the Utah Jazz. It also gave them another NBA title.

The key to Michael Jordan's success is hard work. He never takes anything for granted. He is rich and famous, but he still loves to compete.

Michael has led the NBA in scoring ten times. That's more than any other player. He's the only player to be named to the NBA All-Defensive First Team nine times. That says a lot about his attitude.

He wants to be the best in every aspect of the game. In fact, his teammates say he practices harder than anyone else. The oldest and wealthiest Chicago Bull is the first player at the gym every day. He's also the last to leave.

That's why he's the greatest athlete in history.

Joe Layden is a former newspaper columnist and editor. He has written more than a dozen sports books for kids. His daughter, Emily, says he has a pretty good hoops game—"for an old guy."

Accomplishments: Michael Jordan

Member of NCAA championship team: 1982

Olympic gold medalist: 1984, 1992

NBA Rookie of the Year: 1985

NBA Most Valuable Player: 1988, 1991, 1992, 1996, 1998

Member of NBA championship team:
1991–1993, 1996–1998

Chicago Bulls' all-time leading scorer with 29,277 points

Did you like this book?

Here are two other books from the READ 180 Paperback Collection that you might like to read:

MICHAEL JORDAN

When he was a boy in North Carolina, Michael Jordan dreamed of being a sports star. But he could never have dreamed how successful he would become. Here's the story of one of the most amazing athletes of all time.

BY CHIP LOVITT

THE GOOD FIGHT: STORIES ABOUT REAL HEROES

A young woman risks her life to save her friends. A 12-year-old boy protests child labor. A man puts his life on the line to save the rain forest. These people and other amazing leaders are featured in this book.

BY TOD OLSON

Glossary

accomplishment   something one has achieved

achievement   something one has done successfully

agent   someone who is hired to set up business agreements or other plans

aggressive   forceful

arrogant   conceited and too proud

assist   when a player helps a teammate pass, score points, or make a goal

asthma   a condition that causes difficulty in breathing

awkward   not able to relax and speak to people easily

badminton   a game similar to tennis in which players use rackets to hit a light object called a shuttlecock back and forth over a high net

brutal   cruel

celebrity   a famous person